T0285130

in
the
temple

Catherine
Bagnall &
L. Jane Sayle

in
the
temple

MASSEY UNIVERSITY PRESS

Contents

John Weeks

for C-B

The wind is flying through the French doors
and the garden disappears
if you approach it the wrong way

Sadness is everywhere
but it's not everything
said one of those annoying girls
who notice everything

And where is the velvet landscape
that I might go there
and bide awhile?

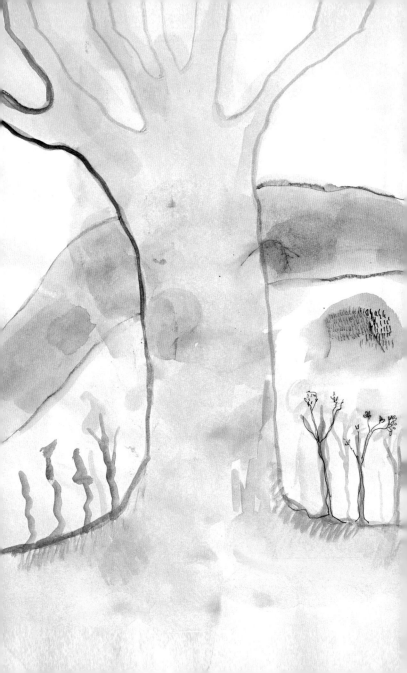

G.P.S.

Walking the narrow path
from Mākara to Ōpau Bay
between the bushy hills
and the shingle beach
it came to me
that there might be someone there
who has lost their way
that no-one else
could show them how to get back
and that I must help them

A handsome diver passes
striding along the path
the wet hessian sack on his back is filled
I know
with blue-boned butterfish
and pāua the colour of wet black ink

How is it that
I hardly need to look around
to know where I am
where the spirited air
invisibly holds
everything in its place

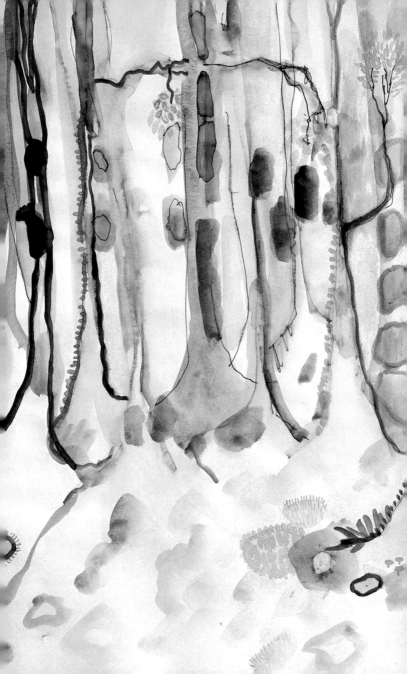

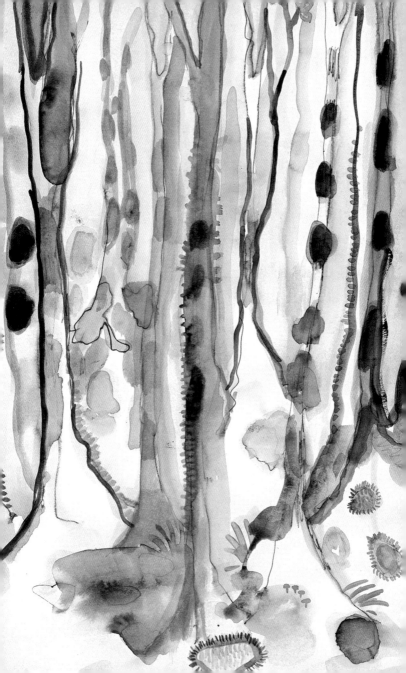

Future Past

Today I planted the grey reeds
by the front door
painted it mauve

Now it's a quiet autumn evening
in the backyard
and I'm burning a chair

Jack Kerouac's rough young voice
comes out from the dark kitchen
he's saying: 'I remember a girl'

And I'm thinking
I'm thinking
I never would have thought this
and
'What will happen?'

Night Walk

Out of nowhere
and after a long flat time
we see a frieze town
of moonlight and liquorice
materialise up ahead

And a brimming harbour
a glistening dark pool
swelling gently
within itself

The Strait

What to make of the confusing clouds
over the long-ago bay
this morning?

The misty mountains
are not that far behind them

But what of all the years
and the cold unpredictable sea between

Falling slowly
in all quietness
down through the air
between tall trees
to a clearing
and bright-sawn firewood
neatly stacked

Back from the clouds of Magellan
the house invisible
near by

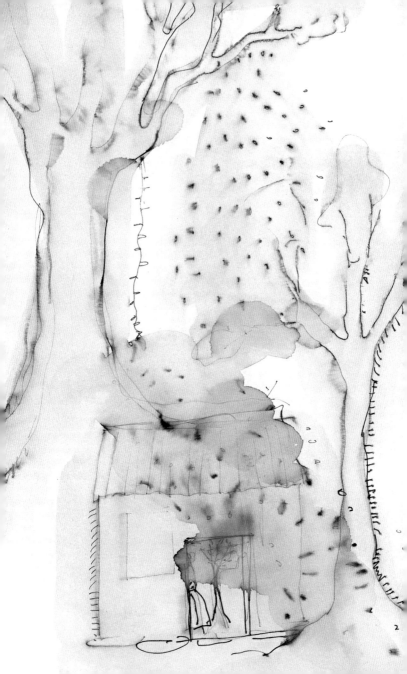

Nightfall

As apples ripen
in the gardens down below
the big house slips its moorings
and floats away over the Southern sea

Keep the pink evening sky on your right
steady as she goes
and head for the land of ice

The sycamores
dance shadows on blank paper
without meaning to

How slow they are to green
as the wild southerly blows!

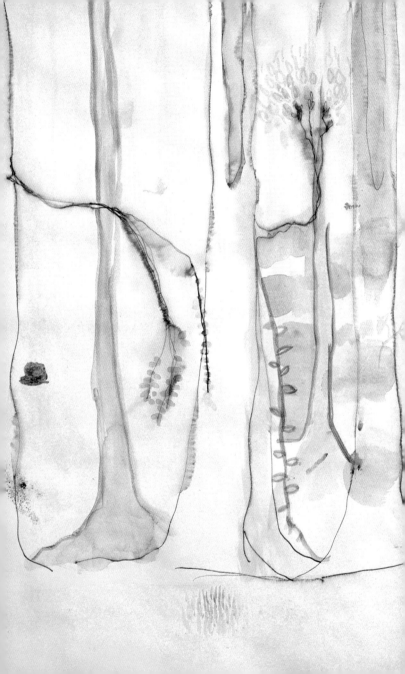

Five Ancestor Poems

Iron Age

I walked into the forest
I walked for two months
and still hadn't cleared it
marvellous yes
but not world enough

Condensation

The castle was made of wood
and the hounds flowed from it
like water down the hill

Dressed in velvet
I see how we lived our lives
all in the fullness of the old moment

The Wrong Camouflage

An admiral alights
on the tall white pillar

Aubade

Two small lights
and a love of old wood
in the spirit house
this navy morning

Old Town

I can't hear myself think
for the whales
singing in the harbour

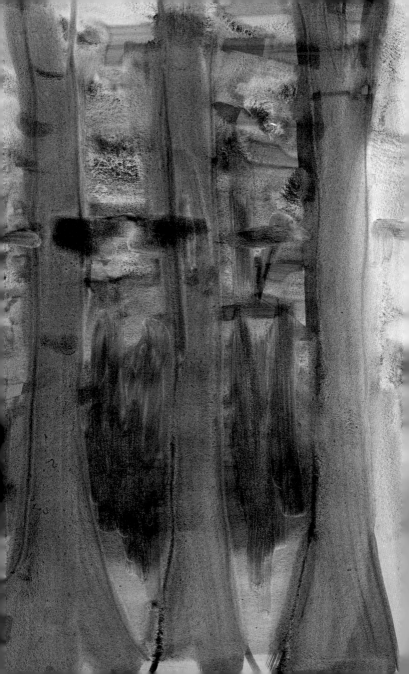

Space Flight

My father is transported
by little girls
skipping along the pavement
outside his window

For nightmares he said
there are fairies on the left side
and the right I forget
expanding into blackness anyway

These empty days all spaces
running up and down stairs
birds are just birds
and it's only the evening sky

Not the day
or the night
and not the stars
not the stars

When her mother died
she felt a trickle of joy
and words formed themselves
inside her head
now she can't see me anymore

But it passed
and now she thinks
about other things
unloved children
and dangerous sea voyages

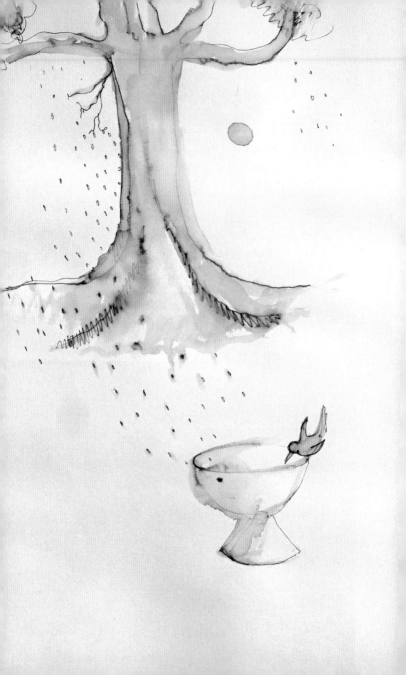

Englischer Garten

No-one noticed my brother
cutting down a tree
with his chainsaw
but a great wind had blown up
and all the detectives in the small city
were on edge

Down by the river
milky water is flowing steadily
and the branches of the chestnut trees
brought low with blossom
refresh themselves

Meanwhile
elsewhere
she is on the scene already

wrinkling her brow
her eyes are glazed
as she soaks up the scene
Wondering how it all fits together

Where Venice Is

A Canaletto sky
glows behind the broken fortifications
on the crest of the dark hill

In the valley
evening smoke drifts up from a chimney
and fantails flicker their silhouettes
against tiers of white weatherboard

.

Journeys

Thousands of swallows flying south
fall invisible
into a field of dry grass

From Florence you wonder
what happened to Italy
it was so hard to get there
and now look

As for me
even if I could swim in the black lake
I'd still take the night flight to India
it's been real

Spy Notes

With my smile
I can go anywhere
yet here I am at twilight
crossing a sodden field alone
to meet someone
who turns out to be you

I'd given up long ago
along with everyone else
but you'd flourished
and grown large
enough to block out the sun
Oh your luminous face!

In the deep-shadowed lamplight
of the derelict barn
I'm losing track of all my stories

Let me begin again
put your arm round my shoulder
and walk out with me
into the chill unremarkable morning

My Military Training

Let's run away!
No, we'll wait
walk away
and sparkle for all time

The Water Snake

I stayed for so long
here for you
it's time to be free of it
my darling

To the water she said
taken by the wind
and trailing the sky
the sun burning
the desert behind us

Nablus

In the Turquoise hostel
sleep in safety and comfort

The stained glass will throw colours
over your sleeping body

Paradise Valley

Walking back to the hut
bright moss underfoot
a dead rabbit in each hand

The silvery glade
in the moonlight

oh the silvery silvery glade!

In the Temple

Afternoons are spent sleeping
mornings in the swirl of herself
just weather

They'll tell you anything
people
all their secrets
just to fill the silence

If it wasn't for
the smell of honeysuckle
the newly summer day

In Camellia Time

It was so late
and your solitude
was like a puppy drowning

Scroll White

And when I close my eyes
black shagreen

Tant le Desire

Some bright red cord
with special knots
and dark remembering blood

Come on little girl
what have you got in you?

A rabbit of gold
incandescent
in the setting sun

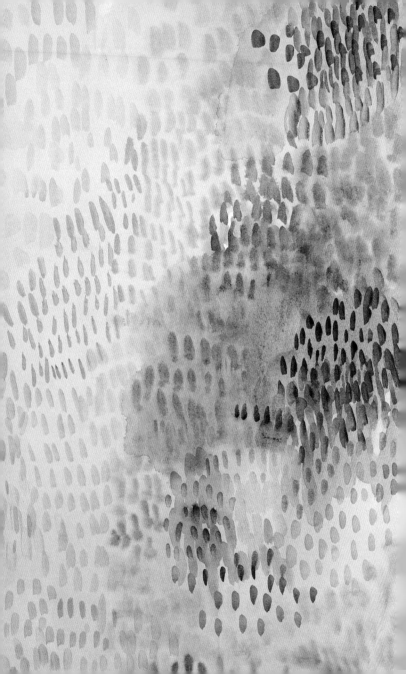

As When

for G.C.

A dog like no other
materialises before you
with its yearning obedient muzzle
and vague antique penis
a Poet's dog

So did the superheroes
chained at the rowlocks
rowing and rowing
dream awake
of sleeping greatness
and soft warm fur

The Singing Tree

Thank you for your poem
I think I understand it
it's just that with the watermarks
the old buff paper
your scrawl

Oh Hod, my Hod,
my voile rose
my Hod,
with you alive is power
you are gently

For there is a leafless winter tree
along whose brown branches
hide small motionless brown birds
and they sing their hearts out
as if the tree itself were

walnut

Gasteranthus extinctus

That being so
by the edge of a deep
fast-flowing river
beset with waterfalls
ridged dark green leaves
shining because of the water
and brilliant orange flowers
shaped like small parrot beaks

List of works

Gloves and ears and waiting, 2022
ink on sketchbook page

Dragonflies in Gollans Valley, 2022
watercolour on sketchbook page

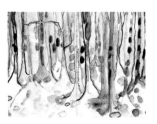

Mahoe, 2022
watercolour on sketchbook page

Beech leaves falling on the tiny hut, 2022
ink on sketchbook page

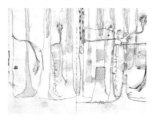

Kohekohe, 2022
watercolour on sketchbook page

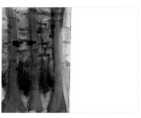

Night, 2022
watercolour on sketchbook page

Air, 2022
watercolour on sketchbook page

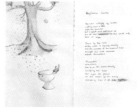

Thoughts about ceramic bird baths, 2022
ink on sketchbook page

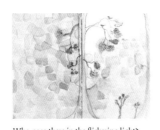

Who goes there in the flickering light?
2022
watercolour on sketchbook page

Friend ships and whispering and dragon flies, 2022
watercolour and pencil on
sketchbook page

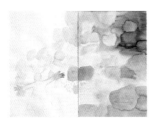

Weather, 2022
watercolour on sketchbook page

What we saw in Paradise Valley, 2022
watercolour on sketchbook page

Beech, 2022
watercolour and pencil on
sketchbook page

Bird song, 2022
watercolour and ink on sketchbook
page

Painted thoughts, 2022
watercolour on sketchbook page

Animal girls drinking at the creek, 2022
watercolour on sketchbook page

Untitled, 2022
watercolour on sketchbook page

Young girl with rabbit and golden light
2022
watercolour on sketchbook page

Untitled, 2022
watercolour on sketchbook page

Pencil study, 2022
pencil on sketchbook page

The ferryman, 2022
watercolour on sketchbook page

75

About the artist

CATHERINE BAGNALL grew up on the bushy eastern shore of the inner Wellington Harbour, where her interest in mythological worlds and enchanted natural spaces began. Inspired by Rosi Braidotti's theories of the post-human and especially the idea of 'a new love of the world', Catherine's work depicts the twenty-first century life of non-human creatures and forest-dwelling girls in the wild green places of the natural living world. She says: 'I think trees are so utterly important — I worship them.' A recognised experimental watercolourist, maker of objects and performance artist, she also lectures in fashion, art and design.

About the poet

L. JANE SAYLE grew up on the south coast of
Wellington. She has been a dealer in curios and
ephemera, an art writer and reviewer, a lecturer in the
history of New Zealand visual culture and a traveller.
In 2021, collaborating with Catherine Bagnall, she
published *On We Go*, a book of poems and paintings
exploring personal connections with the natural world
in the context of the feminine sublime.

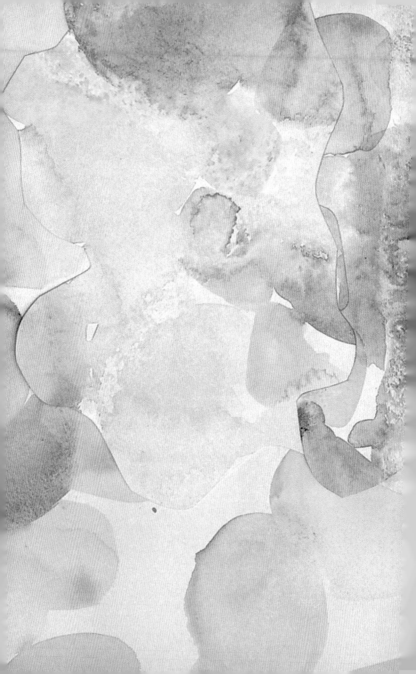